Codependent No More

A Journey to Boost Self-Esteem, Discovering
Healthy Relationships, and Freeing Yourself
from Toxic Patterns

Lori Allen

"Embrace the journey of breaking free from the toxic melody of codependency. Start pleasing yourself, cultivate self-love, and care for your own well-being. Put yourself first and learn the art of healthy detachment. It's time for a better, more loving relationship—with yourself."

\- Lori Allen

TABLE OF CONTENTS

CHAPTER ONE

My Codependency Tale

On the college rollercoaster, I ran into a guy who was three years older than me and a little more seasoned in the ways of the world. Love developed amid lecture halls and late-night pizza parties. I jumped into the deep end of relationships fresh out of high school, unaware of the muddy seas ahead.

We survived the storms of college life together, blossoming in love among textbooks and cafeteria dinners. We weren't just a couple by graduation; we were a team, a "us." The next logical step? Tying the knot.

Marriage, I believed, was the grand step into adulthood. I had no idea I was going to enter a web of emotional reliance, financial dependence, and a type of love that seemed more about 'we' than 'me.'

It's strange how you can get married and still feel like you're a passenger on someone else's trip.

Reality slammed into me like a sledgehammer: this marriage was not the lovey-dovey story I'd anticipated. He was emotionally manipulative, lazy, and had a tendency to prioritize himself. Slowly but steadily, I realized I wasn't just married; I was entangled in a web of codependency.

Breaking free became my mission, but it wasn't easy. First and foremost, I had to admit that I had a problem. My happiness seemed to be linked to him, my wallet served as his personal ATM, and what about my sense of self? It was, after all, on permanent leave.

To get out of this predicament, I had to face up to his emotional games. It felt like I was learning a completely new language, one in which 'no' became my most powerful word. I needed to reconstruct my identity piece by piece, reclaiming elements of myself that I'd voluntarily given up in the name of love.

The divorce papers were more than simply legalese; they were also my proclamation of freedom. The sound of chains snapping rang throughout the courtroom, my battlefield. I was breaking links with a life that had become more about survival than living.

But here's the dramatic twist: liberation wasn't all rainbows and sunshine. Everyone else seemed to be playing happy families, while loneliness and despair disrupted the party. When I compared my path to theirs, it felt like I was running a marathon while they were riding the merry-go-round.

Nonetheless, with each lonely night, I gained strength. Solitude became an ally, an opportunity to discover who I truly was without the weight of other people's expectations. Laughter, which had previously served as a shared soundtrack, gave way to the wonderful symphony of me doing my own thing.

Three years after saying "I do," we said our final farewells. The divorce was the beginning of a new book, not merely the end of a chapter. I was no longer a character in someone else's story; I was the creator of my own.

This isn't just a story about a failed marriage; it's about emerging from the ashes of codependency. The scars are not regrets, but rather mementos of fights won. When I relate my experience, I'm not simply sharing; I'm also passing out flashlights to individuals who are lost in the darkness of codependency.

I hope my story is of assistance to anyone attempting to break free. It is not about divorce;

rather, it is about regeneration. I emerged from the ashes like a phoenix, and now the song of my independence is the only tune I dance to.

*　　　*　　　*　　　*

But, shall we explore deeper into the aftermath?

My life looked like a war zone in the aftermath of my divorce. The wreckage of a shattered marriage surrounded me, and cleaning up the pieces seemed impossible. But, hey, life is a scribbled canvas, and sometimes you have to embrace the mess to create something fresh.

Loneliness became a daily companion of mine. The hole in my heart was reflected by the silence in the vacant spaces. It was a far cry from the shared laughter and whispered promises that used to fill those rooms. Nights were the most difficult—the solitude, a haunting song of what once was.

Comparisons became the ghosts that followed me around during the day. Friends proudly displayed their happily-ever-afters, replete with beaming wives and cooing infants. Meanwhile, I was navigating the single life, ducking intrusive questions and putting on a fake grin. Everyone else looked to be on the fast track to happiness, while I was stranded in the slow lane, staring at a road map that seemed to lead nowhere.

The journey through depression was an emotional rollercoaster. Some days, I felt like I was on the rise, hoping that things would improve. Other days, I descended into depression, wondering every decision that had brought me to this point. It was a battle between self-doubt and a gleam of hope hidden deep within.

But in the darkness, I discovered my own light. Loneliness was transformed into a chance for self-discovery. I began to pick up the bits of myself that had been neglected in the name of 'us.' Hobbies that I had forgotten about were rediscovered, and new passions were developed. The echoes of my laughter gradually filled the empty spaces, creating a melody of newfound delight.

The game of comparison? I flung it out the window. Life is not a race, and happiness does not come in one size fits all. I began setting my own goals, appreciating tiny triumphs, and reveling in the freedom to be myself, with no ties attached.

It wasn't an overnight metamorphosis, but the clouds of despair began to lift gradually. Every stride forward was a victory, no matter how tiny. Therapy became my safe haven, a tool for untangling the emotional knots of the past. It was a path of healing, where wounds became badges of strength.

Then something unexpected happened: love found me again. It was different this time. It was not the result of dependency or a desire for approval. It was a love that sprouted from the fertile ground of self-love, a love that complemented rather than completed.

Life after codependency was a raw and true experience, not a fantasy ending. I stumbled and fell, but I also got back up. The phoenix that rose from the ashes was more than just a survivor; it thrived. The road from codependency to emancipation became the complete tale of my life, which I now offer in the hope that it will serve as a lantern for those who are lost in the dark.

So, here's to a life free of codependency that is messy, beautiful, and wholly mine.

CHAPTER TWO

Understanding Codependency

What is Codependency?

Codependency is a delicate dance of entwined lives, a complicated web that has the power to entangle even the most robust spirits and the strongest of hearts. We must examine the depths of relationships, emotions, and the delicate skill of losing oneself in the pursuit of love to piece together this complex tapestry and come to an understanding of it.

Imagine this: two people who, albeit having different qualities and shortcomings, come together for the sake of love. It appears to be the ideal marriage at first, a partnership in which the two become one. But behind the surface, codependency—a quiet force—begins to define the parameters of their relationship.

See yourself in a relationship where your partner's happiness is your only motivation. Your mood is determined by their feelings, and your sense of value is closely linked to their acceptance. This, my friend, is the essence of codependency: a situation in which one person's needs and wants take precedence over their own sense of self.

Codependency is essentially a psychological and emotional disorder that encourages an unhealthy dependence on other people for identity, approval, and a sense of purpose. It's a relationship dynamic that makes it difficult to distinguish between you and your spouse, resulting in a symbiotic bond that may impede personal development.

The idea of self frequently becomes secondary when codependency is at its worst. The person loses sight of their own needs, wants, and limits because they are so entwined with their relationship. Similar to combining two puzzle pieces, the whole picture is frequently lost to create the appearance of unity.

How did this elaborate dance come about? Usually, within the family, early relationships are where codependency first emerges. It can be influenced by situations in which one or more family members display dominating tendencies, engage in addictive habits, or struggle with mental health concerns. Future codependent habits may be rooted in an environment where emotional needs are disregarded and individuality is stifled during childhood.

Codependency frequently begins innocently enough. The stage is set by a need to connect, to feel loved and welcomed. The heady mixture of love and infatuation in the early stages of a relationship might mask the faint indications of codependency. Who wouldn't want to be near the one they love, after all? But as the partnership develops, the dynamics could change and the once-wholesome bond could turn into something more subtle.

An overly strong dependence on outside validation is one of the characteristics of codependency. The codependent person prioritizes their partner's acceptance and affirmation over their own wants and well-being. Since the partner becomes the main source of one's self-esteem, any perceived rejection or disapproval can cause a codependent to experience severe emotional distress.

Boundaries—or the absence of them—are crucial to codependency. Boundaries are like invisible fences that help maintain a healthy balance between being close to someone and having your own space in a good relationship. These lines become porous in a codependent dynamic when feelings of obligation, guilt, or desertion-related dread obscure them. Saying "no" becomes an enormous challenge because the codependent person thinks that putting limits in place will damage their relationship.

Encouraging behaviors frequently take root in codependent relationships. At the expense of their own well-being, the codependent partner could get sucked into a loop of saving, mending, or meeting the wants of the other. The impulse to be the hero, the unfailing pillar of support, stems from an underlying fear of being left behind and the conviction that one's value is dependent on one's capacity to provide for others.

Codependency is a complex phenomenon that is further woven together by a lack of communication. Suppression of one's actual thoughts and feelings might result from a fear of confrontation and disagreement. The codependent person becomes an expert at placating others, putting harmony ahead of sincerity. If you don't talk about your needs, it can lead to bitterness and disappointment.

Codependency frequently conceals behaviors of manipulation and control. Codependency can appear in both the giver and the receiver, despite the seeming paradox. Motivated by a need for approval, the codependent person may use deceptive methods to manipulate their partner's behavior or feelings. Conversely, they can end up in partnerships with people who behave in a domineering manner, which would continue a destructive cycle.

To escape the grip of codependency, one must delve deeply into self-awareness. It necessitates a readiness to face painful realities and cut the bonds holding you to habits that are impeding your development. Regaining your sense of self, establishing your independence again, and learning to walk the tightrope between connection and individuality are all part of the path.

Determining codependency is a complex process that frequently calls for reflection and a readiness to question deeply held ideas. It entails identifying behavioral patterns, investigating the reasons behind deeds, and realizing how the relationship affects one's emotional health.

A crucial sign of codependency is the inclination to put other people's needs before one's own. Do you frequently struggle to say no, even when it means sacrificing your personal well-being? Do you feel that your value is dependent on your capacity to meet the demands of others, leading you to become unduly involved in their repair or rescue?

The fear of being by oneself is another warning sign. Codependent people would do anything to avoid being alone; they need constant company to keep them from feeling empty within. An ingrained dread of being abandoned or unworthy may be reflected in anxiety at the thought of being independent and self-reliant.

A clear indicator of codependency is the deterioration of personal boundaries. If you frequently find yourself putting your partner's needs and wants ahead of your own, or if you feel like you can never set boundaries, it may be a sign that codependent dynamics are at work.

In the absence of aggressive communication, codependency frequently flourishes. If you feel uncomfortable talking about your genuine feelings and thoughts, or if you value harmony over authenticity, it's time to look at your relationship's communication habits. Codependency can develop from unmet needs and unresolved problems.

The need for approval from others is a recurring element in codependency. If you find that your value comes from other people's acceptance, especially from your partner, you should seriously consider the causes of this dependency. Positive self-talk should come from the inside out, not from outside validation.

Liberating oneself from codependency requires self-compassion and self-discovery; it is not a straight line. Redefining the story of your relationship with yourself and others, facing the fears and beliefs that feed these dynamics, and delving into the origins of codependent patterns are all necessary.

The development of self-awareness is an essential component of this journey. This entails a thorough examination of your feelings, ideas, and actions regarding your relationships. It's about revealing the unconscious patterns that underpin your relationships by removing the layers of conditioning.

A useful friend in the fight to overcome codependency is therapy. A trained therapist can give a secure environment for investigation as well as guidance, resources, and tactics for resolving the intricacies of codependent relationships. Counseling is a brave step toward healing and self-discovery, not a sign of weakness.

Establishing sound boundaries is essential to kicking codependency in the teeth. This entails recognizing and expressing your needs as well as knowing where you stop and your spouse starts. It involves learning to say no when it's necessary and realizing that putting limits in place is a sign of self-love rather than selfishness.

Liberating oneself from codependency entails transforming one's self-esteem via independent validation. This entails accepting your innate value, appreciating your abilities and successes, and developing self-validation skills. It involves recreating the story that characterizes who you are.

Breaking codependent tendencies requires assertive communication skills development. This entails being honest and clear in how you communicate your needs, wants, and views. It entails being open to vulnerability, establishing reasonable expectations, and encouraging candid communication in your relationships.

Acquiring the skill of accepting isolation is a potent remedy for codependency. It's an opportunity to develop a close relationship with oneself and go on a journey of self-discovery. Being alone doesn't always equate to being lonely; solitude may be a place for introspection, creativity, and personal development.

Be kind to yourself as you set out on the path to overcome codependency. Healing is an ongoing process of self-discovery and development rather than a destination. Appreciate the little things in life, learn from them, and know that each step you take ahead is an indication of your perseverance.

To sum up, codependency is a complex web weaved through interpersonal connections. It's a dance that you might miss until the music shifts and the deft movements that have formed the dynamic become apparent. Peeling back the layers, recognizing the patterns, and accepting the path of self-discovery and liberation are all necessary to comprehend codependency. It's a story that can be revised, a tune that can be changed, and an adventure that ends with self-discovery.

Patterns of Codependency

Codependency is a sophisticated dance that is woven throughout relationships. These stages are fluid transitions rather than set milestones that are frequently influenced by our relationships, experiences, and self-discovery moments.

Let's examine each stage in detail, identify the commonalities, acknowledge the challenges, and welcome the transforming potential that results from realizing and conquering codependency. Let's walk this meandering route together to better relationships and the rediscovery of our true selves.

Early Attachments and Conditioning

Early family life is frequently when codependency begins in the tale of our relationships with others. This phase lays the groundwork for more intricate patterns to emerge later.

Consider it this way: our families influence our perceptions of love, trust, and connection when we are young. In my situation, addressing the substance problem took precedence over emotional needs due to a family history of addiction. We came to realize that we had to pretend everything was fine, even if it meant suppressing our emotions.

This unspoken guideline guided me as a child, and I always tried to maintain the appearance of normalcy, especially when it came to a family member who was struggling with addiction. It turned into a manner of life, akin to a dance in which I had to prove my love by allowing things to happen.

In the throes of addiction, roles became confused. There were no obvious boundaries between the person providing care and the person receiving it. Helping others and maintaining a false sense of security while ignoring the underlying issues became entangled with love.

This initial phase involves a complex combination of fear and loyalty, loyalty to the addict and their family, as well as a worry that everything would come to an end if the truth were revealed. I became adept at disguising my true feelings and maintaining appearances by constantly donning a mask. This subsurface codependency was fostered by our fear of being judged by others.

For me, the language of addiction turned into a secret code. Words could not express the silence that appeared to speak for itself, and my expectations of myself were entwined with the family's demands. My feelings alternated between attempting to maintain order and having a persistent fear that everything would break down. Codependency evolved into a way of life rather than merely a means of survival.

When I think back, one day in particular sticks out—the one when everything was on the verge of collapsing. The barricades we'd put up began to crumble as the family member struggling with addiction entered a crisis. I discovered that I was trying to hold everything together by ignoring reality rather than dealing with it head-on. Codependency, which had been managing our lives in the background, came to the fore at that point.

I ended up attempting to deflect and keep things peaceful instead of confronting the problem. My fear of things going wrong kept me back, and codependency had me like a puppet. Beneath the surface, the true demands were concealed by maintaining the appearance of normalcy.

In retrospect, that episode seems to have been a microcosm of the larger story of codependency. It demonstrated my strong need to be in charge of how things appeared, my dread of having to face unpleasant truths, and the silent compromise I had to make between being obedient and taking care of myself—all symptoms of my early attachments and training stage.

This is not unique to me; many families struggling with addiction or mental health issues experience similar things. Feelings turn into a maze of unfulfilled desires, hidden agreements, and a never-ending attempt to maintain stability.

Let us examine this initial phase of codependency with empathy and comprehension. People frequently develop codependent behaviors amid family life as a coping mechanism for difficult situations. It's a strategy for overcoming obstacles rather than a decision.

Regaining control at this early stage requires careful planning. It entails being aware of the taught behaviors, accepting the influence of family dynamics, and practicing self-compassion while attempting to make changes.

In my path, I was able to start changing when I realized that codependency wasn't just a part of who I was. It's like realizing that I've learned how to manage things not so well and that I can now learn how to do it better.

Enabling and Denial

Behaviors play a secondary role in enabling. It's similar to downplaying the seriousness of the situation, covering up for someone, and making excuses. You may find yourself trying to mediate conflicts by keeping things seeming ideal when they're not.

This dance involves a lot of denial. It's like looking at everything through magnifying glasses. You may believe that the other person's behavior is just peculiar and that your discomfort is the result of your oversensitivity. It's a means of projecting an illusion of perfection onto the connection when there are actually rifts on the surface.

Usually, the dance between denial and enabling begins with the best of intentions. Even while your intentions may be good—to assist or maintain order—this can become a vicious cycle in which you unwittingly encourage bad behavior. It's similar to becoming entangled in a web of maintaining an immaculate appearance but gradually losing some of your individuality.

Usually, the realization that this dance of enabling and denial has permeated the partnership deeply serves as a wake-up call. What you once believed to be affection and caring begins to feel like chains securing you to an unhealthy world.

For me, things were complicated early in my marriage. There were hints here and there that something fishy was going on, including my husband's subtly oppressive behavior. Rather than drugs being the source of the issues, it was more about him manipulating his thoughts.

He was skilled at creating the impression that everything in our relationship was fine. In reality, though, it resembled a play in which we were both characters. Because the deception was initially disguised as love and concern, I didn't see it clearly.

His behavior appeared innocent at first, but as time went on, I saw a pattern of control slipping in. I let him get away with things for too long, believing our relationship was perfect when it wasn't.

I had an idealistic view of the world, believing that his behavior was peculiar and that my discomfort was the result of my oversensitivity. I was living in denial, thinking our relationship was flawless while in reality it was a little messed up.

It was like making excuses for him and downplaying what he was doing when you allowed his manipulative behavior. I turned into a peacemaker, gradually sacrificing my independence in the process of attempting to maintain perfection.

The realization that the deception was intricately entwined with our relationship served as a wake-up call. The things that I mistakenly believed to be love were actually binding me to a dystopian reality that confused control and compassion.

Facing the emotional maze in our relationship was necessary to get us out of this problem. I had to face the difficult truth, peel back the layers of denial, and acknowledge the subliminal control strategies. It was difficult and made me realize how much it had affected my mental health. Our bond required a significant adjustment.

Lack of Boundaries

This is like standing on shaky ground when it becomes difficult to distinguish between oneself and other people. It's a stage characterized by brittle boundaries when a compulsive fixation on the wants and needs of others replaces personal autonomy. A complicated web of codependent behaviors, frequently entangled with emotional manipulation, sloth, and narcissism, flourishes from this lack of defined limits.

This phase showed up subtly but profoundly in the complex tapestry of my own codependent path. It felt like there was an unseen force field around me, telling me to submit to my husband's whims over my wants. His ability to manipulate emotions was akin to a deft magician using sleight of hand to deflect my focus from my own desires to his ongoing emotional maintenance.

My inability to say no was blatant evidence of my lack of limits. The concept of "no" felt strange to me and endangered the fragile balance I was trying so hard to keep. Without boundaries, this one-sided dynamic continued, whether it was me putting up with his demands even at the price of my own needs or repressing my emotions to keep things peaceful.

The absence of limits was a tacit consent to travel over the rough seas of his emotional terrain without using my own compass. It required giving up both physical and emotional privacy on the altar of codependency. The walls that ought to have protected my identity started to leak, letting the emotional blackmail creep in like a slow-acting poison.

I remember a vivid incident that perfectly captures the emotional manipulation and lack of boundaries that characterized this stage. I was caught up in a web of obligation and remorse on what seemed to be a routine evening. Using a well-constructed story, my husband described how his difficult day had left him feeling devastated by my absence.

Without sound limits, I took on the role of emotional caregiver, trying to repair the wounds that life had inflicted on him. It was a deft use of subtle but effective emotional manipulation, one that made me feel bad for voicing my own desires. Refusing to comply seemed like defiance, a departure from the part I had unintentionally taken on in our mutually beneficial relationship.

Boundaries were not respected in the domain of personal space either. His narcissistic characteristics and laziness took center stage, seeking his praise and attention all the time. Whether it was giving in to his every whim or walking carefully on his thin ego, my identity was subordinated to the unrelenting quest of preserving the precarious balance of our relationship.

The height of the emotional blackmail occurred during arguments. Whenever I tried to voice my wants or my displeasure, I was met with a deft performance of guilt and finger-pointing. Rather than being a shield, boundaries turned into combat zones where my aspirations of independence were quickly destroyed.

I felt helpless because of this lack of boundaries, thinking that my value depended on meeting his emotional needs. At this point, his emotional orbit had a stronger gravitational pull on me than my own goals and ambitions. The barriers that were supposed to protect my uniqueness crumbled, leaving me with a hollow feeling and a need for approval.

The absence of boundaries in the larger framework of codependency is a duet in which both partners participate. When there are no clear boundaries, the emotional manipulator might thrive and take advantage of the codependent person's weakness. It's a mutually beneficial dance in which the codependent dynamic is sustained by a cycle in which one partner's lack of boundaries supports the other's deceptive strategies.

Releasing ourselves from this stage required a radical change of viewpoint. It required appreciating the importance of boundaries as protectors of identity and self-worth. Setting up healthy boundaries required a self-discovery process and the reclaiming of space that had been freely given up in the name of love.

It took reflection and a willingness to question long-held assumptions about my place in the relationship for me to go on this life-changing path.

It meant realizing that healthy limits are not walls but rather avenues for genuine connection, and it meant learning to say no without feeling guilty.

Codependency's lack of boundaries stage is a sobering reminder of how crucial self-preservation is. During this stage, a person may feel trapped or as though their emotional demands are taking over them due to the breakdown of their personal boundaries. My personal experience serves as evidence of the transforming power of acknowledging and reclaiming boundaries, which is an essential first step in escaping the bonds of codependency and regaining one's inner strength.

Loss of Self Identity

The phase of codependency known as "lack of boundaries" is like standing on shaky ground when it becomes difficult to distinguish between oneself and other people. It's a stage characterized by brittle boundaries when a compulsive fixation on the wants and needs of others replaces personal autonomy. A complicated web of codependent behaviors, frequently entangled with emotional manipulation, sloth, and narcissism, flourishes from this lack of defined limits.

This phase showed up subtly but profoundly in the complex tapestry of my own codependent path. It felt like there was an unseen force field around me, telling me to submit to my husband's whims over my wants. His ability to manipulate emotions was akin to a deft magician using sleight of hand to deflect my focus from my own desires to his ongoing emotional maintenance.

My inability to say no was blatant evidence of my lack of limits. The concept of "no" felt strange to me and endangered the fragile balance I was trying so hard to keep. Without boundaries, this one-sided dynamic continued, whether it was me putting up with his demands even at the price of my own needs or repressing my emotions to keep things peaceful.

The absence of limits was a tacit consent to travel over the rough seas of his emotional terrain without using my own compass. It required giving up both physical and emotional privacy on the altar of codependency. The walls that ought to have protected my identity started to leak, letting the emotional blackmail creep in like a slow-acting poison.

I remember a vivid incident that perfectly captures the emotional manipulation and lack of boundaries that characterized this stage. I was caught up in a web of obligation and remorse on what seemed to be a routine evening. Using a well-constructed story, my husband described how his difficult day had left him feeling devastated by my absence.

Without sound limits, I took on the role of emotional caregiver, trying to repair the wounds that life had inflicted on him. It was a deft use of subtle but effective emotional manipulation, one that made me feel bad for voicing my own desires. Refusing to comply seemed like defiance, a departure from the part I had unintentionally taken on in our mutually beneficial dance.

Boundaries were not respected in the domain of personal space either. His narcissistic characteristics and sloth took center stage, seeking my praise and attention all the time. Whether it was giving in to his every whim or walking carefully on his thin ego, my identity was subordinated to the unrelenting quest of preserving the precarious balance of our relationship.

The height of the emotional blackmail occurred during arguments. Whenever I tried to voice my wants or my displeasure, I was met with a deft performance of guilt and finger-pointing. Rather than being a shield, boundaries turned into combat zones where my aspirations of independence were quickly destroyed.

I felt helpless because of this lack of boundaries, thinking that my value depended on meeting his emotional needs. At this point, his emotional orbit had a stronger gravitational pull on me than my own goals and ambitions. The barriers that were supposed to protect my uniqueness crumbled, leaving me with a hollow feeling and a need for approval.

The absence of boundaries in the larger framework of codependency is a duet in which both partners participate. When there are no clear boundaries, the emotional manipulator might thrive and take advantage of the codependent person's weakness. It's a mutually beneficial dance in which the codependent dynamic is sustained by a cycle in which one partner's lack of boundaries supports the other's deceptive strategies.

Releasing ourselves from this stage required a radical change of viewpoint. It required appreciating the importance of boundaries as protectors of identity and self-worth. Setting up healthy boundaries required a self-discovery process and the reclaiming of space that had been freely given up in the name of love.

It took reflection and a willingness to question long-held assumptions about my place in the relationship for me to go on this life-changing path. It meant realizing that healthy limits are not walls but rather avenues for genuine connection, and it meant learning to say no without feeling guilty.

Codependency's lack of boundaries stage is a sobering reminder of how crucial self-preservation is. During this stage, a person may feel trapped or as though their emotional demands are taking over them due to the breakdown of their personal boundaries.

My personal experience serves as evidence of the transforming power of acknowledging and reclaiming boundaries, which is an essential first step in escaping the bonds of codependency and regaining one's inner strength.

We are similar to detectives in that we try to figure out how we became enmeshed in codependency. It's like turning on a light in the somewhat perplexing realm of our relationships when we recognize these patterns.

It's the first major step in escaping the quagmire of codependency. It's like discovering a map that enables us to alter the narratives of our own and, more significantly, interpersonal interactions.

This chapter serves as our guide onward, just like that initial spark. Finding the patterns is not as important as applying that understanding to improve our relationships and rediscover our authentic selves. As we examine these patterns, let's keep in mind that altering the entire codependency narrative and having the courage to truly observe what's happening are the first steps toward being free.

CHAPTER THREE

Codependent Relationships

Here, we'll explore how to spot codependent patterns in relationships, offering a roadmap for self-reflection and understanding. In the world of connections, it's easy to miss the subtle signs that we might be caught in the web of codependency.

Together, we'll navigate the fine line between healthy support and getting too entangled, understand the art of setting boundaries, and explore the give-and-take of emotions in relationships.

Recognizing these patterns is like decoding a hidden language—one that speaks of unmet needs, fuzzy boundaries, and the quest for individuality within the tapestry of partnership.

So, let's dive into this journey together, peeling back layers to reveal the subtle complexities that shape our connections.

Signs and Indicators

Within the complexities of relationships, specific cues can indicate the existence of codependency, which is a dynamic in which an individual's identity is entangled with the wants and needs of another. Let's explore these subliminal indicators that frequently pass unnoticed, illuminating the complex web of codependent relationships.

Overemphasis on the Other

It's common in codependent relationships to put the needs and wants of the other partner above one's own. This frequently shows itself as an unwavering emphasis on making sure the other person is happy and well, sometimes at the expense of one's own needs.

Jenny consistently neglected her own goals and wants in favor of her husband's demands. His contentment became a gauge of her value, which caused her identity to gradually erode.

Difficulty Setting Boundaries

Well-defined boundaries are essential to healthy partnerships; yet, codependency causes these limits to become hazy. People may find it difficult to speak up for themselves because they frequently worry about getting into a fight or losing someone they love.

Fearing that turning down his partner's wishes would damage their relationship, Mark found it difficult to say no. He took on obligations that were above his capabilities as a result of his lack of boundaries, which left him in a state of perpetual overload.

Severe Fear of Abandonment

Codependent people frequently have a deep-seated dread of being turned away or rejected. This dread may motivate actions meant to prevent the other person from withholding their love or acceptance.

Because she was afraid of being abandoned, Sarah put up with actions from her spouse that were harmful to her well-being. Even at the expense of her happiness, she held onto the connection.

Diminished Personality

The distinctions between distinct identities may become hazy in codependency. When they put their significant other's interests, goals, and values above their own, the codependent spouse may lose sight of their own.

Once ardent about his hobbies, Michael eventually gave them up to conform to his partner's interests. His identity eventually dwindled to being a mirror image of the person he was seeing.

People-Pleasing Behaviors

People-pleasing tactics are frequently used by codependents to win others over and steer clear of conflict. This may entail holding down one's actual emotions and ideas, which prevents the relationship from being honest.

Even when Lisa disagreed with her partner, she found herself agreeing. She suppressed her voice out of fear of conflict and disagreement, compromising her authenticity to maintain the appearance of unity.

Difficulty in Self-Care

Setting one's health first is essential to a happy partnership. Codependent people may find it difficult to take care of themselves because they are preoccupied with the needs of the other person.

James was so preoccupied with meeting his partner's requirements that he ignored his own physical and mental health. He had prioritized keeping the partnership over his personal needs, so the idea of self-care sounded alien to him.

Victim and Rescuer Dynamics

Codependent partnerships frequently display victim-rescuer dynamics. To keep the other spouse in a cycle of dependence, one partner may adopt the role of continuously saving the other from difficulties or issues.

Emma experienced a feeling of approval after saving her partner's finances. But this dynamic covered up more serious problems in their relationship and prevented each partner from dealing with their problems.

Sensitivity to Emotions

Those who are codependents may react more strongly emotionally to their spouses' feelings and moods. The codependent's emotional health starts to depend on how the other person is feeling.

When his spouse was upset, Alex experienced a wave of anxiety. He became extremely watchful in an attempt to keep the connection emotionally stable, frequently at the expense of his emotional stability.

Conflict Avoidance

Relationships inevitably involve conflict, but codependency frequently exhibits a dislike of it. People will do all in their power to avoid conflict because they believe that it will inevitably result in rejection.

Chris kept his worries to himself to keep the peace appear genuine. Open communication was hampered by the dread of disagreement, which impeded the relationship's development.

Having Trouble Accepting Help

Those who are codependent could find it difficult to accept assistance or support from others because they see it as a sign of weakness. This resistance is frequently the result of the conviction that one must be independent to be respected.

Rachel's relationship was difficult, but she refused to go to treatment. Accepting outside help went against her deep-rooted conviction that she should be able to manage things on her own.

Recognizing these indicators is an essential first step in escaping the codependency web. It's a call to introspection and a compass pointing people in the direction of better relationship dynamics. Let's investigate these signs and set off on an empowerment and awareness path, where identifying these patterns serves as a trigger for constructive change.

CHAPTER FOUR

Relationship Assessment Tools

Self Reflection Exercise

Spend a moment reflecting on the dynamics of your relationships with thoughtfulness. The purpose of this activity is to help you identify codependent patterns and gain an understanding of your emotional terrain.

Identifying Priorities:

Think about how you allocate your time and emotional resources in your relationships. Consider if you frequently put your partner's needs and wants ahead of your own. Ask yourself:

1. How often do I find myself prioritizing the needs of my partner over my own?

2. Do I feel bad for expressing my needs or wants?

Boundary Exploration:

Explore the idea of setting limits in your relationships. Consider how well you can establish and uphold boundaries. Ask yourself:

1. Is it easy for me to let my spouse know what my boundaries are?
2. Do I experience dread or worry when I think about setting limits?

Emotional Dependence:

Evaluate your emotional autonomy in the partnership. Consider if there is a degree of emotional blending between you and your partner that could be a sign of codependency. Ask yourself:

1. Do I feel in charge of overseeing my partner's emotional health?
2. Is it possible for me to tell the difference between my partner's and my feelings?

Conflict Resolution Patterns:

Examine the processes you and your partner use to resolve disputes. Consider if there is a propensity to steer clear of conflict or if disputes are handled in a positive, healthy way. Ask yourself:

1. How do I usually handle disagreements with my partner?
2. Am I hesitant to voice my actual sentiments and opinions when we disagree?

Assessment of Personal Identity:

Consider how much of your personality you can preserve in the partnership. Think about whether your objectives, passions, and dreams are supported. Ask yourself:

1. Do I feel that my partner's goals frequently take precedence over mine?
2. How successfully do I keep being myself in the relationship?

Needs and Validation:

Consider how validation functions in your partnership. Consider whether you need other people's approval, especially from your partner, to feel worthy of yourself. Ask yourself:

1. To what extent does my partner's approval affect my sense of worth?
2. Do I look to my partner for approval or assurance all the time?

Enabling Behaviors:

Think about if you participate in enabling actions that could prolong harmful patterns in the relationship. Think back to the times you might be saving your significant other from the fallout from their deeds. Ask yourself:

1. Do I frequently find myself saving my partner from difficulties or obligations?
2. To what extent am I at ease with my partner taking responsibility for their decisions?

As you negotiate the complicated terrain of your emotions and relationships, take your time with these reflections and practice self-compassion. Instead of self-judgment, the aim is self-awareness, which opens the door to development and the formation of more wholesome, harmonious relationships.

Codependency Checklist

Instructions: Give a sincere response to each of the following questions while considering your experiences in previous and present relationships. To evaluate the existence and degree of codependent patterns, refer to the scoring guide provided at the conclusion.

1. **Do you find it difficult to establish and uphold personal boundaries in your partnership?**

Score:
- ☐ 0 - Rarely
- ☐ 1 - Sometimes
- ☐ 2 - Often
- ☐ 3 - Almost Always

2. **Do you find it difficult to tell your partner "no" or to communicate your needs?**

Score:

- ☐ 0 - Rarely
- ☐ 1 - Sometimes
- ☐ 2 - Often
- ☐ 3 - Almost Always

3. **Do you constantly feel that you need your partner's validation or approval?**

Score:

- ☐ 0 - Rarely
- ☐ 1 - Sometimes
- ☐ 2 - Often
- ☐ 3 - Almost Always

4. **Do your decisions in the relationship stem from a fear of being left out or abandoned?**

Score:

- ☐ 0 - Rarely
- ☐ 1 - Sometimes
- ☐ 2 - Often
- ☐ 3 - Almost Always

5. **Are your partner's tastes or wishes the main factors influencing the important decisions you make in life?**

Score:

- ☐ 0 - Rarely
- ☐ 1 - Sometimes
- ☐ 2 - Often
- ☐ 3 - Almost Always

6. Do you feel compelled to put your partner's objectives ahead of your own?

Score:

- ☐ 0 - Rarely
- ☐ 1 - Sometimes
- ☐ 2 - Often
- ☐ 3 - Almost Always

7. Do you have trouble telling your lover how you feel?

Score:

- ☐ 0 - Rarely
- ☐ 1 - Sometimes
- ☐ 2 - Often
- ☐ 3 - Almost Always

8. Do you often repress your emotions to keep the peace in the relationship?

Score:

- ☐ 0 - Rarely
- ☐ 1 - Sometimes
- ☐ 2 - Often
- ☐ 3 - Almost Always

9. Do you regularly find yourself saving your significant other from the repercussions of their behavior?

Score:

- ☐ 0 - Rarely
- ☐ 1 - Sometimes
- ☐ 2 - Often
- ☐ 3 - Almost Always

10.Is there a pattern of covering up your partner's behavior to protect them?

Score:

- ☐ 0 - Rarely
- ☐ 1 - Sometimes
- ☐ 2 - Often
- ☐ 3 - Almost Always

11.Do you think your partner's hobbies, aspirations, and identity have eclipsed your own?

Score:

- ☐ 0 - Rarely
- ☐ 1 - Sometimes
- ☐ 2 - Often
- ☐ 3 - Almost Always

12.Is there a loss of sense of self in the relationship?

Score:

- ☐ 0 - Rarely
- ☐ 1 - Sometimes
- ☐ 2 - Often
- ☐ 3 - Almost Always

Scoring Guide:

0–9: Codependency is unlikely.

10–18: Moderate signs of codependent behaviors. Think about studying these processes in more detail.

19–27: Codependency is present in a moderate amount. For relationships to function better, these tendencies must be evaluated and addressed.

27–36: Codependency is very likely. It is advised to seek out expert advice and assistance to navigate and overcome these tendencies.

Recall that this checklist serves as a self-reflection tool rather than a conclusive diagnostic. If your results point to possible codependency, think about consulting a therapist or counselor to learn more about these dynamics.

CHAPTER FIVE

Strategies for Breaking Free

Breaking free from the bonds of codependency is a transformative path toward self-discovery and autonomy in the complex dance of relationships. This chapter serves as a resource for techniques that will enable you to take back your identity, establish sound boundaries, and cultivate relationships that will support rather than undermine you.

Let's review the fundamentals of codependency before we get into escape tactics. It's a pattern of relationships in which the emotional and psychological needs of two people entwine, frequently to an unhealthy degree. Acknowledging this relationship is the initial stride towards freedom.

Awareness and Self-Reflection

Develop self-awareness as the first step on your quest. Consider your feelings, ideas, and actions in connection to your relationships. What are my wants and desires in this relationship? is a question to ask oneself. You create the groundwork for escaping codependency by deliberately considering your reasons and reactions.

Determining Healthy Boundaries

The cornerstones of a healthy partnership are boundaries. To safeguard your well-being, start by determining your requirements and establishing obvious limits. This entails telling your partner what your boundaries are.

- Using "no" when appropriate.
- Prioritizing self-care without guilt.

Proper boundaries establish a balanced dynamic that promotes understanding and respect for one another.

Building Independence

Find your uniqueness again and develop a feeling of freedom. This includes:

- Reestablishing connections with activities and hobbies that make you happy.
- Aiming for your own objectives and dreams.
- Maintaining relationships and friendships outside of your main partnership.

The secret to escaping the entanglements of codependency is independence.

Successful Communication Techniques

Open and Honest Communication: Develop an open and honest communication approach. To foster vulnerability and understanding, openly express your ideas and emotions.

Make use of "I" statements: Use "I" statements to voice your demands and concerns to prevent placing blame and promote a cooperative conversation. Say, "I feel overwhelmed when..." as an example, rather than "You always..."

Active Listening: Use active listening techniques to comprehend your partner's viewpoint. This entails:

- Maintaining eye contact.
- Making verbal affirmations.
- Observing your partner's expressions.

Set Communication Goals: Work with your partner to establish specific goals for communication. This could entail talking about:

- Effective ways to communicate needs and boundaries.
- Techniques for settling disputes amicably.
- The value of honest communication in preserving a happy partnership.

One of the most important things in breaking codependent habits is effective communication.

Therapeutic Support

Consulting a therapist or counselor can offer priceless perspectives and strategies for overcoming codependency. Expert assistance provides:

- A secure environment for delving into more profound feelings.
- Methods for enhancing dialogue.
- Techniques for enhancing personal resilience.

Therapy is a proactive step on the road to recovery and development.

Self-Care and Mindfulness

Include mindfulness exercises in your routine to improve stress management and self-awareness. This can involve:

- Deep breathing exercises and meditation.
- Partaking in enjoyable and soothing activities.
- Making self-care a priority in your routine.

Being mindful helps you connect with yourself and your needs on a deeper level.

Educate Yourself

Acquiring knowledge is an effective means of overcoming codependency. Learn about:

- Healthy dynamics in relationships.
- Codependent behaviors and their consequences.
- Methods for achieving and preserving independence.

Knowing the dynamics at work gives you the ability to make wise decisions.

Accepting Liberation

The process of overcoming codependency is transformational and calls for dedication, introspection, and an openness to change. You can start along the path to happier, healthier relationships by developing self-awareness, setting up appropriate boundaries, and placing a high value on clear communication.

Recall that breaking free from codependency is an ongoing process rather than a destination. Celebrate the little things as you use these tactics, and remember to be kind to yourself. You are getting closer to a relationship based on respect for one another, personal development, and the ability to be who you truly are with every deliberate step you take.

CHAPTER SIX

Coping with Loneliness

An experience with loneliness is a profound reality that frequently arises after escaping the web of codependency. Even though it can be difficult, this feeling is a necessary ally on the road to self-discovery and creating stronger bonds with others. Together, we will embrace the transforming path that lies ahead and manage the complexities of coping with loneliness after releasing ourselves from codependency.

Embracing Solitude

Although loneliness can initially seem like a vast, barren landscape, it's important to recognize the difference between isolation and loneliness. Being alone is a deliberate decision; it's a place where you make time to be with yourself.

Accept this time of seclusion as a chance for introspection. Take part in happy and fulfilling activities, reviving interests and passions that were previously obscured by codependent relationships.

Rebuilding Connections

Isolation may not always follow from loneliness. It gives you a blank canvas on which to reconstruct and reinterpret your social ties. Find family, friends, or new acquaintances who share your changing self-concept. As you surround yourself with people who value and celebrate your path, you will cultivate relationships founded on respect and understanding for one another.

Self-Compassion

It takes a lot of self-compassion to deal with loneliness. Recognize the power that comes from navigating the complexities of your emotions and the fortitude it needs to overcome codependency. Be nice to yourself and remember that loneliness is a temporary feeling that passes on the road to recovery.

Fostering Independence

Take advantage of your alone time to develop your independence and self-sufficiency. Discover how to make choices based on your goals, inclinations, and desires. You may change loneliness from a void to a place where personal growth can occur as you gradually develop this sense of autonomy.

Explore New Relationships

Being alone can be a call to make new friends. But approach this investigation mindfully, cognizant of the changing you. Select partnerships that enhance your well-being and are consistent with your values.

Accept the possibility of deep relationships that will enhance your just-acquired freedom.

Nurturing Inner Contentment

In addition to being a journey toward coping with loneliness, inner fulfillment is the goal. Think about your goals, your basic beliefs, and the person you are growing into. The sensation of loneliness on the outside turns into a friend rather than an enemy as you take care of your inner self, leading you to connect with your true aspirations.

Acknowledging Emotional Waves

Like all emotions, loneliness comes in waves. Let go of judgment and allow yourself to surf these waves. While some days could be difficult, others might feel easygoing. Recognize that emotional fluctuations are a normal component of the healing process. Accept the lessons they have to teach and recognize the power of taking them head-on.

Seeking Professional Assistance

It's brave to seek professional assistance if loneliness overwhelms you. Counselors and therapists can give a secure environment for discussing the causes of loneliness and can also provide advice on coping mechanisms. An invaluable tool for negotiating the emotional terrain following codependency release is professional assistance.

Creating a Support System

When loneliness is shared with others, it fades. Build a network of people who understand and are there for you on your journey. Communicate your feelings, ideas, and experiences to support groups or close friends. Expressing yourself helps people connect with you and reaffirms that you are not alone in your challenges.

Patience and Self-Discovery

Overcoming loneliness requires a marathon of self-discovery rather than a sprint. Recognize that healing takes time and exercise patience throughout the process. Make the most of your time alone to uncover aspects of yourself that the dynamics of codependency may have obscured. When faced patiently, loneliness can catalyze deep self-discovery.

Creative Expression

Take up artistic endeavors as a way to deal with loneliness. Use art, writing, music, or any other medium to communicate your feelings; find a creative outlet for your feelings. This is a tangible reflection of your journey toward emotional freedom in addition to offering a therapeutic release.

Acts of Gratitude

When you're feeling lonely, remember to be grateful. Pay attention to the areas of your life that provide you happiness, contentment, and a feeling of direction. Gratitude creates an attitude of gratitude for the path you are on by changing the focus from what is lacking to what is abundant.

Embracing Change

Accepting change is inextricably linked to overcoming loneliness. Understand that overcoming codependency is a transforming process that calls for changes in attitudes, actions, and interpersonal dynamics. Accept the way your life is changing and be willing to adapt to it, knowing that it will always be a part of your journey towards personal development.

Having a connection to nature

The spirit can be profoundly soothed by nature. Spend time outside, take in the splendor of the environment, and let the peace of nature soothe your loneliness. The intricacies of emotional landscapes stand in stark contrast to the simplicity of nature.

Mindfulness Practices

Make mindfulness exercises a part of your everyday routine. These techniques help you stay grounded in the here and now, whether they are done through walking mindfully, deep breathing exercises, or meditation. Being mindful helps you recognize loneliness without passing judgment on it, which makes it easier for you to deal with this feeling.

Setting Personal Goals

Being alone might be a chance to establish and work on personal objectives. Set goals that correspond with your interests and ambitions. These objectives serve as sources of inspiration in times of loneliness in addition to giving one a feeling of direction. Honor each step you take to reach these objectives.

Thoughts on Dependency

Take advantage of your loneliness to engage in thoughtful reflection as you work to overcome codependency. Recognize the progress made since breaking free and comprehend the patterns that brought you to this place. In addition to strengthening self-awareness, reflection serves as a compass for ongoing personal growth.

Social Engagement

Take part in social events that are related to your hobbies. Join groups, go to events, or take part in get-togethers in the neighborhood to meet people who share your interests. Making genuine relationships through social interaction helps to reinforce your newly acquired independence.

Establishing Rituals

Establish weekly or daily rituals to give your life shape and regularity. Establishing these routines—whether they be morning, evening, or weekly activities—brings a reassuring element to the alone and promotes self-care and stability.

Journaling

Write down your feelings and ideas in your journal. Putting
your thoughts, experiences, and goals on paper creates a physical archive of your path. Writing in a journal gives you a therapeutic outlet and helps you

to reflect and make sense of the complicated issues surrounding loneliness.

Connecting with Spirituality

Investigate spirituality as a way to connect and find comfort. Reaching out to your spiritual side, whether via meditation, religious practice, or philosophical inquiry, provides a significant source of solace and comprehension.

CHAPTER SEVEN

My Ongoing Journey

After escaping the complex maze of codependency, life was like a blank canvas ready to be filled in with fresh colors. Every day was a unique combination of growth opportunities, obstacles, and the thrilling quest to uncover my true self.

The once-dreadful prospect of solitude becomes a chance for personal growth. I was able to investigate my tastes, dreams, and desires when I was alone myself. It feels like dancing to my tunes and relishing in my individuality.

After the divorce, life was like picking up the broken parts of a vase. Although it wasn't simple, every broken shard taught us a valuable lesson. Rebuilding allowed me to create a new image of myself, not just put things back together.

Friends turned into the support that helped me get by in the post-codependency environment. The void left by a partnership that prioritized reliance over connection was filled with their sincere chats and laughing.

Independence, the lone dance of self-reliance, evolved into a festivity of individual development. Developing new hobbies and rekindling old ones was like creating my choreography. Every stride served as a statement of liberation.

What was once a storm of loneliness became a sea I could sail. I used solitude as a blank canvas for reflection and as a way to get in touch with my inner self. The quiet before a life-changing realization was provided by loneliness rather than being a curse.

Comparisons were erased, along with the demons of my past. I realized that happiness isn't a gauge of one's own and that life isn't a race. Accepting my special journey served as a springboard for my successes.

A dark journey, depression evolved into an investigation of one's value. Even though there were difficult days, therapy developed into a secure haven for releasing emotional tangles and encouraging a healing mindset.

Once more, love found me, but it wasn't the same. It arose out of self-love rather than desperation. Without any ties to reliance, it enhanced my life.

Creating new benchmarks turned into a custom for acknowledging modest successes. Every choice I made, from redefining relationships to embracing isolation, was a reflection of my changing ideals.

Not only did the phoenix emerge from the ashes of codependency, but it flourished. Life after codependency was a real, gritty story of self-discovery rather than a happily ever after.

My goal is to serve as a beacon of hope for others who are still lost as I go on. Scars are maps of battles fought and won, not regrets. This ongoing narrative is a beacon of hope for anyone trying to break free from the web of codependency—it's not just mine.

The theme of emancipation continues to play in the symphony of my life. Savoring the subtle nuances of self-discovery and resilience rather than rushing to a destination is the goal of the journey beyond codependency.

More colorful strokes are added to the canvas every day, creating a picture of honesty and independence that is a monument to the resiliency of the human spirit and the potential for resurrection from the ashes of codependency.

Break Free, Embrace You

Own Your Journey, Love

"Come on, embrace the beautiful, messy process of self-discovery. We discover strength in our weaknesses, and we can inspire others with our tales. May your path be filled with chapters that resonate with the resilience in us all"

\-   Lori Allen